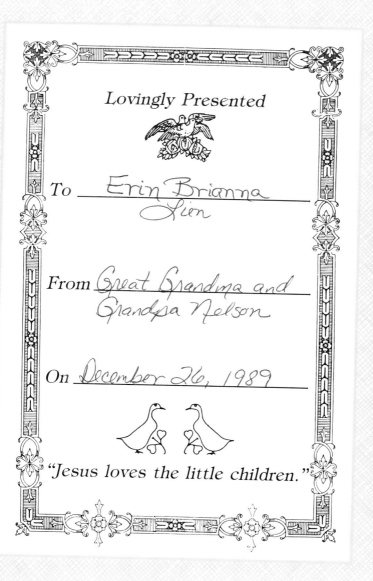

Lovingly Presented

To _Erin Brianna Lien_

From _Great Grandma and Grandpa Nelson_

On _December 26, 1989_

"Jesus loves the little children."

With special thanks to my dear friend, Chris Francis,
for her loving assistance in the preparation of this book.

**ISBN** 0-529-06481-2

Copyright© 1987 Marjorie Decker

❖❖❖❖❖❖❖❖❖❖❖❖❖❖❖❖❖❖❖

Published by
WORLD BIBLE PUBLISHERS, INC.
Iowa Falls, Iowa

CHRISTIAN MOTHER GOOSE®

# Rock-A-Bye
## ❧ Bible ☙

Selected Scripture from
The Authorized King James Version

☙❧

with
Favorite Rhymes from
The Christian Mother Goose® Books
by

# Marjorie Ainsborough Decker

# THAT YOU MAY KNOW . . .

The heart and purpose of this special book is to bring to precious children refreshing sips of Scripture, served from a "storybook glass" made of favorite rhymes from the World of Christian Mother Goose.®

You will find great truths from classical passages of God's Word. They stand majestically alongside the simplicity of a rhyme written and illustrated for little hearts and minds to readily relate these great truths to their own childlike world.

All of our lives have been touched by children. Many of us have set the life-course of these eager, little ships who have trusted us to set their sails on a true course. God Himself has provided the water and the wind.

I join my prayer with yours that the Rock-A-Bye Bible will gently invite each tender heart to "desire the sincere milk of the word, that ye may grow thereby," and to "grow in grace and in the knowledge of our Lord and Savior Jesus Christ."

*Marjorie Ainsborough Decker*

## LITTLE SHIP

Little ship, I set your sail
  To follow with the winds of God
The course of life The Son of God
  Has laid for you, today.

Little ship, I place aboard
  Your compass and your sacred chart:
God's Word to guide your tender heart
  From sea to sea, each day.

Little ship, the flag you fly
  Flies bravely o'er the waves below;
It bears the Name of Jesus, so
  Your course is safe in Him.

Little ship, sail on, sail on;
  Bring home a cargo, rich and true,
To Him Who gives the Light and Life to you
  To sail; sail on!

    Little ship . . .
      Little ship . . .
        Sail with God!

And there were in the same country shepherds abiding in the field, keeping watch over their flock by night.

And, lo, the angel of the Lord came upon them, and the glory of the Lord shone round about them: and they were sore afraid.

And the angel said unto them, Fear not: for, behold, I bring you good tidings of great joy, which shall be to all people.

For unto you is born this day in the city of David a Savior, which is Christ the Lord.

And this shall be a sign unto you; Ye shall find the babe wrapped in swaddling clothes, lying in a manger.

—Luke 2:8-12

## LITTLE BOY BLUE

Little Boy Blue,
Come blow your horn,
The sheep's in the stable
Where the Savior is born.
Where is the boy
Who looks after the sheep?
Watching Baby Jesus,
Fast asleep.

The Lord is my shepherd; I shall not want.

He maketh me to lie down in green pastures: he leadeth me beside the still waters.

He restoreth my soul: he leadeth me in the paths of righteousness for his name's sake.

Yea, though I walk through the valley of the shadow of death, I will fear no evil: for thou art with me; thy rod and thy staff they comfort me.

Thou preparest a table before me in the presence of mine enemies: thou anointest my head with oil; my cup runneth over.

Surely goodness and mercy shall follow me all the days of my life: and I will dwell in the house of the Lord for ever.

— Psalm 23

## MARY'S LAMB

Mary had a little lamb,
Its fleece was white as snow,
And everywhere that Mary went
The lamb was sure to go.
Now, Jesus has a little lamb,
That little lamb is you!
And He is pleased
When all His lambs
Keep following Him, too.

esus answered . . . Whosoever drinketh of this water shall thirst again:

But whosoever drinketh of the water that I shall give him shall never thirst; but the water that I shall give him shall be in him a well of water springing up into everlasting life.

—John 4:13,14

If any man thirst, let him come unto me, and drink.

He that believeth on me, as the scripture hath said, out of his belly shall flow rivers of living water.

—John 7:37,38

And the Spirit and the bride say, Come. And let him that heareth say, Come. And let him that is athirst come. And whosoever will, let him take the water of life freely.

—Rev. 22:17

## JACK AND JILL

Jack and Jill went up the hill
To fetch a pail of water.
A man there said,
"If you drink this,
You'll still be thirsty after.
But there is water Jesus gives,
So won't you ask Him first,
To give you LIVING WATER
So that you will never thirst."
Up Jack got and home did trot,
A whole mile and a quarter,
To tell the GOOD NEWS
To his friends,
About God's LIVING WATER.

**W**hen I fall, I shall arise . . .

—Micah 7:8

Though he fall, he shall not be utterly cast down: for the Lord upholdeth him with His hand.

—Psalm 37:24

For I will restore health unto thee, and I will heal thee of thy wounds, saith the Lord.

—Jer. 30:17

Arise, go thy way: thy faith hath made thee whole.

—Luke 17:19

The spirit of the Lord God is upon me; because the Lord hath anointed me to preach good tidings unto the meek; He hath sent me to bind up the brokenhearted, to proclaim liberty to the captives, and the opening of the prison to them that are bound.

—Isa. 61:1

For with God nothing shall be impossible.

—Luke 1:37

## HUMPTY DUMPTY

Humpty Dumpty sat on a wall,
Humpty Dumpty had a great fall;
Humpty Dumpty shouted, "Amen!
God can put me together again."

For the Son of man is come to save that which was lost.

How think ye? if a man have an hundred sheep, and one of them be gone astray, doth he not leave the ninety and nine, and goeth into the mountains, and seeketh that which is gone astray?

And if so be that he find it, verily I say unto you, he rejoiceth more of that sheep, than of the ninety and nine which went not astray.

Even so it is not the will of your Father which is in heaven, that one of these little ones should perish.

—Mat. 18:11-14

## LITTLE BO-PEEP

Little Bo-Peep
Has lost her sheep
And doesn't know where
To find them;
But Jesus knows
And can bring them home,
Wagging their tails
Behind them.

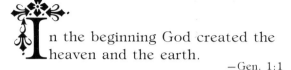 n the beginning God created the heaven and the earth.

—Gen. 1:1

He made the stars also. And God set them in the firmament of the heaven to give light upon the earth,
And to rule over the day and over the night, and to divide the light from the darkness: and God saw that it was good.

—Gen. 1:16-18

And they that be wise shall shine as the brightness of the firmament; and they that turn many to righteousness as the stars for ever and ever.

—Daniel 12:3

## TWINKLE, TWINKLE, LITTLE STAR

Twinkle, twinkle, little star,
God has placed you where you are,
Up above the world so high,
You're God's light hung in the sky.
Twinkle, twinkle, little star,
When you look down from afar,
What's the little light you see
Shining here for God? It's me!
Twinkle, twinkle, little star,
God has placed you where you are.

I heard the voice of the Lord, saying, Whom shall I send, and who will go for us? Then said I, Here am I; send me.

—Isaiah 6:8

Go ye into all the world, and preach the gospel to every creature.

—Mark 16:15

Jesus said, Suffer little children to come unto me, and forbid them not: for of such is the kingdom of God.

—Luke 18:16

Behold, what manner of love the Father hath bestowed upon us, that we should be called the sons of God.

—I John 3:1

For the earth shall be filled with the knowledge of the glory of the Lord, as the waters cover the sea.

—Hab. 2:14

## BOBBY SHAFTOE

Bobby Shaftoe's gone to sea,
To pray upon his little knee
That boys and girls will come to see
That Jesus really loves them.

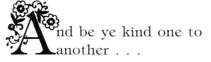

nd be ye kind one to
another . . .

—Eph. 4:32

Add . . . brotherly kindness; and to
brotherly kindness, charity.

—II Pet. 1:7

Be rich in good works, ready to
distribute, willing to communicate.

—I Tim. 6:18

Them that believed were of one
heart and of one soul; neither said
any of them that aught of the things
which he possessed was his own.

—Acts 4:32

They helped every one his neighbor.

—Isaiah 41:6

But be ye doers of the word and
not hearers only.

—James 1:22

## THREE KIND MICE

Three kind mice,
See what they've done!
They helped a lost chick
To find Mother Hen,
They brought some food
To the church mice, then
They cleaned up the tree house
For Jenny Wren,
Those three kind mice.

How beautiful upon the mountain are the feet of him that bringeth good tidings, that publisheth peace; that bringeth good tidings of good, that publisheth salvation; that saith unto Zion, Thy God reigneth!

—Isaiah 52:7

So shall my word be that goeth forth out of my mouth: it shall not return unto me void, but it shall accomplish that which I please, and it shall prosper in the thing whereto I sent it.

—Isaiah 55:11

For after that in the wisdom of God, the world by wisdom knew not God, it pleased God by the foolishness of preaching to save them that believe.

—I Cor. 1:21

## DOCTOR FOSTER

Doctor Foster went to Gloucester
In a shower of rain;
He went to teach,
He went to preach
God's Word, and make it plain.

Thou visitest the earth, and waterest it; thou greatly enrichest it with the river of God, which is full of water; thou preparest them corn, when thou hast so provided for it.

Thou waterest the ridges thereof abundantly; thou settlest the furrows thereof; thou makest it soft with showers; thou blessest the springing thereof.

Thou crownest the year with thy goodness, and thy paths drop fatness.

They drop upon the pastures of the wilderness, and the little hills rejoice on every side.

—Psalm 65:9-12

The flowers appear on the earth.

—S. of S. 2:12

# MISTRESS MARY

Mistress Mary, quite contrary,
How does your garden grow?
God sends rain and sun,
And then one by one
The flowers pop up in a row.

I will lift up mine eyes unto the hills, from whence cometh my help.

My help cometh from the Lord, which made heaven and earth.

He will not suffer thy foot to be moved: He that keepeth thee will not slumber.

Behold, He that keepeth Israel shall neither slumber nor sleep.

The Lord is thy keeper: the Lord is thy shade upon thy right hand.

The sun shall not smite thee by day, nor the moon by night.

The Lord shall preserve thee from all evil: he shall preserve thy soul.

The Lord shall preserve thy going out and thy coming in from this time forth, and even for evermore.

—Psalm 121

26

## ROCK-A-BYE, BABY

Rock-a-bye, baby,
On the tree top,
When the wind blows
The cradle will rock;
Mother will make
The baby a shawl;
God will keep baby,
Cradle and all.

**B**ut the very hairs of your head are all numbered.

—Mat. 10:30

But the natural man receiveth not the things of the Spirit of God: for they are foolishness unto him: neither can he know them, for they are spiritually discerned.

—I Cor. 2:14

But God hath chosen the foolish things of the world to confound the wise; and God hath chosen the weak things of the world to confound the things which are mighty;

And base thing of the world, and things which are despised, hath God chosen, yea, and things which are not, to bring to nought things that are.

—I Cor. 1:27-28

## SIMPLE SIMON

Simple Simon met a Pieman
Going to the fair.
Said Simple Simon to the Pieman,
"Can you count your hair?"
Said the Pieman to Simple Simon,
"No one can count hairs, son."
Said Simple Simon to the Pieman,
"God counts them, every one!"

Then Jesus said unto them,
Verily, verily, I say unto you,
Moses gave you not that bread from
heaven; but my Father giveth you the
true bread from heaven.

For the bread of God is He which
cometh down from heaven, and giveth
life unto the world.

Then said they unto him, Lord,
evermore give us this bread.

And Jesus said unto them, I am the
bread of life: he that cometh to me
shall never hunger; and he that
believeth on me shall never thirst.

—John 6:32-35

# HOT CROSS BUNS

Hot cross buns,
Hot cross buns,
One a penny,
Two a penny,
Hot cross buns.
Give them to your daughters,
Give them to your sons,
Tell them Who's The Bread of Life!
Hot cross buns.

I will never leave thee, nor forsake thee.

—Heb. 13:5

Fear thou not; For I am with thee: be not dismayed; for I am thy God; I will strengthen thee; yea, I will help thee; yea, I will uphold thee with the right hand of my righteousness.

—Isaiah 41:10

Behold, I am with thee, and will keep thee in all places whither thou goest.

—Gen. 28:15

Lo, I am with you always, even unto the end of the world.

—Mat. 28:20

### JUMPING JOAN

Here am I,
Little Jumping Joan;
Since Jesus is with me,
I'm not all alone.

Oh that men would praise the Lord for his goodness, and for his wonderful works to the children of men!

For He satisfieth the longing soul, and filleth the hungry soul with goodness.

—Psalm 107:8,9

Therefore I say unto you, Take no thought for your life, what ye shall eat; neither for the body, what ye shall put on.

The life is more than meat, and the body is more than raiment.

Consider the ravens: for they neither sow nor reap; which neither have storehouse nor barn; and God feedeth them: how much more are ye better than the fowls?

—Luke 12:22-24

## LITTLE TOMMY TUCKER

Little Tommy Tucker
Sang for his supper.
What was the song
That he sang
For bread and butter?
"God is so good,
And God cares for little Tom."
That's what he sang
Down to the last crumb.

Your Father knoweth what things ye have need of, before ye ask Him.

After this manner therefore pray ye: Our Father which art in heaven, Hallowed be thy Name.

Thy kingdom come. Thy will be done in earth, as it is in heaven.

Give us this day our daily bread.

And forgive us our debts, as we forgive our debtors.

And lead us not into temptation, but deliver us from evil: For thine is the kingdom, and the power, and the glory, for ever. Amen.

—Mat. 6:8-13

## THERE WAS AN OLD WOMAN

There was an old woman
Who lived in a shoe.
She had so many children
And loved them all, too!
She said, "Thank you, Lord Jesus,
For sending them bread."
Then kissed them all gladly
And sent them to bed.

J esus said unto her, I am the resurrection, and the life: he that believeth in Me, though he were dead, yet shall he live:

And whosoever liveth and believeth in Me shall never die. Believest thou this?

—John 11:25,26

In my Father's house are many mansions: if it were not so, I would have told you. I go to prepare a place for you.

And if I go and prepare a place for you, I will come again, and receive you unto myself; that where I am, there ye may be also.

—John 14:2,3

Surely I come quickly. Amen. Even so, come, Lord Jesus.

—Rev. 22;20

## RING-A-RING O'ROSES

Ring-a-ring o'roses,
A pocket full of posies,
It's true! It's true!
Jesus rose for me and you!

Ring-a-ring o'roses,
A pocket full of posies,
It's true! It's true!
He's coming back
For me and you!

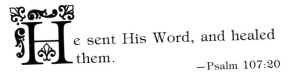

e sent His Word, and healed them.

—Psalm 107:20

I will go before thee, and make the crooked places straight.

—Isaiah 45:2

He giveth power to the faint; and to them that have no might He increaseth strength.

Even the youths shall faint and be weary, and the young men shall utterly fall:

But they that wait upon the Lord shall renew their strength; they shall mount up with wings as eagles; they shall run, and not be weary; and they shall walk and not faint.

—Isaiah 40:29-31

If thou canst believe, all things are possible to him that believeth.

—Mark 9:23

## THERE WAS A CROOKED MAN

There was a crooked man
Who walked a crooked mile.
He never could straighten up,
So never did smile.
He found a little book
That said, "God makes
The crooked straight!"
He believed,
And straightened up with smiles
And jumped the garden gate!

He caused an east wind to blow in the heaven: and by his power he brought in the south wind.

—Ps. 78:26

The wind bloweth where it listeth, and thou hearest the sound thereof, but canst not tell whence it cometh, and whither it goeth: so is every one that is born of the Spirit.

—John 3:8

The fruit of the Spirit is love, joy, peace, longsuffering, gentleness, goodness, faith, meekness, temperance.

—Gal. 5:22,23

The love of God is shed abroad in our hearts by the Holy Spirit which is given unto us.

—Romans 5:5

## I CAN'T SEE THE WIND

I can't see the wind,
But I see what it blows:
Balloons in the air
And Mommy's washed clothes.
I can't see God's Spirit
Blowing down from above,
But I see how He blows
Our home full of His love.

In the beginning was the Word, and the Word was with God, and the Word was God.

The same was in the beginning with God.

All things were made by Him; and without Him was not any thing made that was made.

—John 1:1-3

And God made the beast of the earth after his kind, and cattle after their kind, and every thing that creepeth upon the earth after his kind: and God saw that it was good.

—Gen. 1:25

# BOW, WOW, WOW

Bow, wow, wow,
Whose dog art thou?
Little Tom Tinker's dog,
Bow, wow, wow.

Bow, wow, wow,
Who madest thou?
Little Tom Tinker's God!
Bow, wow, wow.

**B**lessed are ye that sow beside all waters.

—Isaiah 32:20

But this I say, He which soweth sparingly shall reap also sparingly; and he which soweth bountifully shall reap also bountifully.

—II Cor. 9:6

Jesus said . . . learn of me.

— Mat. 11:29

Forasmuch as ye know that ye were not redeemed with corruptible things, as silver and gold,

But with the precious blood of Christ, as of a lamb without blemish and without spot.

—I Pet. 1:18,19

And all thy children shall be taught of the Lord; and great shall be the peace of thy children.

—Isaiah 54:13

## SING A SONG OF SIXPENCE

Sing a song of sixpence,
A pocket for the Lord;
Four and twenty children
A penny could afford
To send across the ocean,
For other children there
To learn about dear Jesus,
Who answers every prayer.

Thy word is a lamp unto my feet, and a light unto my path. The entrance of thy words giveth light; it giveth understanding unto the simple.

—Psalm 119:105, 130

Ye are the light of the world. A city that is set on a hill cannot be hid.

Neither do men light a candle, and put it under a bushel, but on a candlestick; and it giveth light unto all that are in the house.

Let your light so shine before men, that they may see your good works, and glorify your Father which is in heaven.

—Mat. 5:14-16

# LITTLE NANCY ETTICOAT

Little Nancy Etticoat
In a white petticoat,
With a little light
That glows and glows!
Never tries to hide it;
All the town has spied it!
Little Nancy Etticoat's
Little light grows!

And we have known and believed the love that God hath to us. God is love; and he that dwelleth in love dwelleth in God, and God in him.

Herein is our love made perfect, that we may have boldness in the day of judgment: because as He is, so are we in this world.

There is no fear in love; but perfect love casteth out fear: because fear hath torment. He that feareth is not made perfect in love.

We love Him, because He first loved us.

—I John 4:16-19

### IF

If all the world were paper
And seas were ink so blue,
We couldn't write enough to tell
How much that God loves you.

Give, and it shall be given unto you; good measure, pressed down, and shaken together, and running over, shall men give into your bosom. For with the same measure that ye mete withal it shall be measured to you again.

—Luke 6:38

A just weight and balance are the Lord's; all the weights of the bag are His work.

—Proverbs 16:11

But lay up for yourselves treasures in heaven, where neither moth nor rust doth corrupt, and where thieves do not break through nor steal:

For where your treasure is, there will your heart be also.

—Mat. 6:20,21

## BAA, BAA, BLACK SHEEP

Baa, Baa, black sheep.
Have you any wool?
Yes, sir, yes, sir,
Three bags full:
One for my master,
One for the Lord, too,
And one for the little boy
Who says, "Thank you!"

In what place therefore ye hear the sound of the trumpet, resort ye thither unto us: our God shall fight for us.

—Neh. 4:20

And that, knowing the time, that now it is high time to awake out of sleep: for now is our salvation nearer than when we believed.

—Rom. 13:11

## JEREMIAH OBADIAH

Jeremiah Obadiah
Climbed the wall of Nehemiah.
With a trumpet in his hand,
He woke the folk across the land.

And Jesus said unto them, Come ye after me, and I will make you to become fishers of men.

And straightway they forsook their nets, and followed Him.

—Mark 1:17,18

Neither is there salvation in any other; for there is no other name under heaven given among men whereby we must be saved.

—Acts 4:12

I have loved thee with an everlasting love: therefore with loving-kindness have I drawn thee.

—Jer. 31:3

# ONE, TWO, THREE, FOUR, FIVE

One, two, three, four, five,
Once I caught a fish alive;
Six, seven, eight, nine, ten,
Jesus said, "Now, fish for men!"
How can I catch men on a hook?
God tells you how in His Good Book.

**B**ehold, I stand at the door, and knock: if any man hear my voice, and open the door, I will come in to him, and will sup with him, and he with me.

—Rev. 3:20

Because thy lovingkindness is better than life, my lips shall praise thee.

Thus will I bless thee while I live: I will lift up my hands in thy name.

—Psalm 63:3,4

Lift up your heads, O ye gates; and be ye lifted up, ye everlasting doors; and the King of glory shall come in.

Who is this King of glory? The Lord of hosts, He is the King of glory.

—Psalm 24: 7,10

## KNOCK AT THE DOOR

Knock at the door,
Peep in.
Lift up the latch,
Walk in!
Welcome, dear Lord!
Join in.
Lift up our hands,
Praise Him!

nd thou shalt love the Lord thy
God with all thy heart, and
with all thy soul and with all thy
mind, and with all thy strength: this
is the first commandment.

And the second is like, namely this,
Thou shalt love thy neighbor as
thyself. There is none other
commandment greater than these.

—Mark 12:30-31

I was glad when they said unto me,
Let us go into the house of the Lord.

—Psalm 122:1

# A DILLER, A DOLLAR

A diller, a dollar
A ten o'clock scholar,
He's on time for his church school!
He got up early in the morning
To keep the Golden Rule:
"Love the Lord
With all your heart,
And all your playmates, too!"
A diller, a dollar,
A ten o'clock scholar,
God is watching over you!

For God so loved the world, that he gave his only begotten Son, that whosoever believeth in him should not perish, but have everlasting life.

For God sent not his Son into the world to condemn the world; but that the world through him might be saved.

—John 3:16,17

For the Lord himself shall descend from heaven with a shout, with the voice of the archangel, and with the trump of God: and the dead in Christ shall rise first:

Then we which are alive and remain shall be caught up together with them in the clouds, to meet the Lord in the air: and so shall we ever be with the Lord.

Wherefore comfort one another with these words.

—I Thess. 4:16-18

## LAVENDER'S BLUE

Lavender's blue, dilly, dilly,
Lavender's green,
Teach me to say, dilly, dilly,
John 3:16.
God loved the world, dilly, dilly,
He gave His Son,
To give His life, dilly, dilly,
For everyone.

Lavender's blue, dilly, dilly,
Lavender's green,
Here comes the King, dilly, dilly,
In clouds He's seen.
I'll wear my best, dilly, dilly,
My whitest gown,
The King will give, dilly, dilly,
To me a crown.

Praise ye the Lord, Praise God in his sanctuary; praise Him in the firmament of His power.

Praise Him for His mighty acts; praise Him according to His excellent greatness.

Praise Him with the sound of the trumpet; praise Him with the psaltery and harp.

Praise Him with the timbrel and dance; praise Him with stringed instruments and organs.

Praise Him upon the loud cymbals; praise Him upon the high sounding cymbals.

Let everything that hath breath praise the Lord. Praise ye the Lord.

—Psalm 150

## RIDE A COCK-HORSE

Ride a cock-horse
To Banbury Cross,
To see all the children
Make music and sing.
With bells on their fingers
And bells on each toe,
They praise God with music
Wherever they go.

**L**ord, how oft shall my brother sin against me, and I forgive him? till seven times?

Jesus saith unto him, I say not unto thee, until seven times: but, until seventy times seven.

—Mat. 18:21,22

And be ye kind one to another, tenderhearted, forgiving one another, even as God for Christ's sake hath forgiven you.

—Eph. 4:32

For thou, Lord, art good, and ready to forgive; and plenteous in mercy unto all them that call upon thee.

—Psalm 86:5

## TWEEDLEDUM AND TWEEDLEDEE

Tweedledum and Tweedledee
Once had a quarrel;
For Tweedledum said Tweedledee
Had pushed him off a barrel.
Said Tweedledee to Tweedledum,
"I'm very, very sorry."
Said Tweedledum to Tweedledee,
"I'll forgive you in a hurry."

I will praise Thee; for I am fearfully and wonderfully made: marvelous are thy works; and that my soul knoweth right well.

My substance was not hid from thee when I was made in secret, and curiously wrought, in the lowest parts of the earth.

Thine eyes did see my substance, yet being unperfect; and in thy book all my members were written, which in continuance were fashioned, when as yet there was none of them.

How precious also are thy thoughts unto me, O God! How great is the sum of them!

—Psalm 139:14-17

Thus saith the Lord, thy Redeemer, and He that formed thee from the womb, I am the Lord that maketh all things.

—Isaiah 44:24

## YOU ARE SPECIAL

You are very, very special;
There is no one just like you!
God made you just the way you are,
When He specially thought of you.
He wanted so many children,
And not one to be the same,
So that you could be a special you,
With a very special name.
Then to every SPECIAL little girl,
And every SPECIAL little boy,
God has given a SPECIAL HEART
To put His love in to enjoy.

And, lo, the star, which they saw in the east, went before them, till it came and stood over where the young child was.

When they saw the star, they rejoiced with exceeding great joy.

And when they were come into the house they saw the young child with Mary, his mother, and fell down, and worshiped Him; and when they had opened their treasures, they presented unto Him gifts; gold and frankincense, and myrrh.

—Mat. 2:9-11

We would see Jesus.

—John 12:21

## STAR LIGHT, STAR BRIGHT

Star light, star bright,
Guide us on our way tonight;
I wish I may, I wish I might,
See the King this very night.

They shall ask the way to Zion . . . saying, Come, and let us join ourselves to the Lord in a perpetual covenant that shall not be forgotten.

—Jer. 50:5

But ye are come unto mount Zion, and unto the city of the living God, the heavenly Jerusalem.

—Heb. 12:22

Jesus saith, I am the way, the truth, and the life: no man cometh unto the Father, but by Me.

—John 14:6

Therefore the redeemed of the Lord shall return, and come with singing unto Zion; and everlasting joy shall be upon their head.

—Isaiah 51:11

## SEE-SAW, SACARADOWN

See, saw, sacaradown,
Which is the way to Zion town?
Up the narrow way, not down,
That is the way to Zion town.

**P**leasant words are as a honeycomb, sweet to the soul, and health to the bones.

—Prov. 16:24

A word fitly spoken is like apples of gold in pictures of silver.

—Proverbs 25:11

She openeth her mouth with wisdom; and in her tongue is the law of kindness.

—Proverbs 31:26

Set a watch, O Lord, before my mouth; keep the door of my lips.

—Psalm 141:3

Let the words of my mouth, and the meditation of my heart, be acceptable in thy sight, O Lord, my strength, and my redeemer.

—Psalm 19:14

O Lord, open thou my lips; and my mouth shall shew forth thy praise.

—Psalm 51:15

## ONCE I SAW A LITTLE WORD

Once I saw a little word
Come hop, hop, hop;
It wasn't kind at all,
And I cried, "Stop, stop, stop!"
Once I saw a little word
As soft as heather;
I blew it through my lips
And said, "Go on forever!"

**I** am the good shepherd, and know my sheep, and am known of mine.

As the Father knoweth me, even so know I the Father: and I lay down my life for the sheep.

And other sheep I have, which are not of this fold: them also I must bring, and they shall hear my voice; and there shall be one fold, and one shepherd.

—John 10:14-16

He shall feed his flock like a shepherd: he shall gather the lambs with his arm, and carry them in his bosom.

—Isa. 40:11

## SEE-SAW, MARGERY DAW

See-saw, Margery Daw,
Jackie has found a new Master.
His Name is Jesus,
Shepherd and Friend,
And Jackie's a sheep in His pasture.

ow also when I am old and grayheaded, O God, forsake me not; until I have showed thy strength unto this generation, and thy power to every one that is to come.

—Psalm 71:18

Let no man despise thy youth; but be thou an example of the believers, in word, in conversation, in charity, in spirit, in faith, in purity.

—I Tim. 4;12

Having compassion one of another, love as brethren, be pitiful, be courteous.

—I Pet. 3:8

A little child shall lead them.

—Isaiah 11:6

## ONE MISTY, MOISTY MORNING

One misty, moisty morning,
When cloudy was the weather,
There I met an old man
Clothed all in leather.
I put my hand beneath his arm
And helped him through the rain.
He said, "I thank you,
Thank you, child,
And thank you, once again."

ndrew saith . . . there is a lad here, which hath five barley loaves, and two small fishes: but what are they among so many?

And Jesus said, Make the men sit down. Now there was much grass in the place. So the men sat down, in number about five thousand.

And Jesus took the loaves; and when He had given thanks, He distributed to the disciples, and the disciples to them that were set down; and likewise of the fishes as much as they would.

When they were filled, He said unto His disciples, Gather up the fragments that remain, that nothing be lost.

Then those men, when they had seen the miracle that Jesus did, said, This is of a truth that prophet that should come into the world.

—John 6:8-12,14

## PAT-A-CAKE

Pat-a-cake, pat-a-cake,
Baker's man,
Bake me a cake
As fast as you can.
Pat it and prick it,
And mark it with G,
Put it in the oven
For God and me.

**B**lessed be the Lord, who daily loadeth us with benefits, even the God of our salvation.

—Psalm 68:19

The eyes of all wait upon thee; and thou givest them their food in due season.

—Psalm 145:15

Enter into His gates with thanksgiving, and into His courts with praise: be thankful unto Him, and bless His name.

—Psalm 100:4

For every creature of God is good, and nothing is to be refused, if it is received with thanksgiving:

For it is sanctified by the Word of God and prayer.

—I Tim. 4:4,5

## LITTLE MISS MUFFET

Little Miss Muffet
Sat on a tuffet,
Thanking Jesus for curds and whey;
There came a big spider
And sat down beside her,
To listen to Miss Muffet pray.

**B**ut continue thou in the things which thou hast learned and hast been assured of, knowing of whom thou hast learned them;

And that from a child thou hast known the holy scriptures, which are able to make thee wise unto salvation through faith which is in Christ Jesus.

All scripture is given by inspiration of God, and is profitable for doctrine, for reproof, for correction, for instruction in righteousness:

—II Tim. 3:14-16

But these are written that ye might believe that Jesus is the Christ, the Son of God; and that believing ye might have life through His name.

—John 20:31

84

## LITTLE JACK HORNER

Little Jack Horner
Sat in a corner,
Reading his Bible each day;
He learned what it said,
And each night in bed,
The verses he learned he would say.
The first night he said:
"Since God so loved us
We should love one another."
The next night he said:
"Obey Father and Mother."
At the end of the week
He had learned verse seven,
That Jesus is the way to Heaven.

Lo, children are an heritage of the Lord: and the fruit of the womb is his reward.

—Psalm 127:3

And Jesus called a little child unto Him, and set him in the midst of them,

And said, Verily I say unto you, Except ye be converted, and become as little children, ye shall not enter into the kingdom of heaven.

Whosoever, therefore, shall humble himself as this little child, the same is greatest in the kingdom of heaven.

And whosoever shall receive one such little child in my name receiveth me.

—Mat. 18:2-5

## MONDAY'S CHILD

Monday's child will seek God's face,
Tuesday's child is full of grace,
Wednesday's child in faith will grow,
Thursday's child God's love will show,
Friday's child is loving and giving,
Saturday's child thanks God for living,
And the child that is born
On the Lord's first day,
Will trust Him as He leads the way.

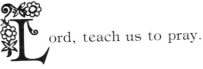

ord, teach us to pray.

—Luke 11:1

But thou, when thou prayest, enter into thy closet, and when thou hast shut thy door, pray to thy Father which is in secret; and thy Father which seeth in secret shall reward thee openly.

—Mat. 6:6

Pray for them which despitefully use you, and persecute you;
That ye may be the children of your Father which is in heaven: for he maketh his sun to rise on the evil and on the good, and sendeth rain on the just and on the unjust.

—Mat. 5:44,45

And all things, whatsoever ye shall ask in prayer, believing, ye shall receive.

—Mat. 21:22

# WEE WILLIE WINKIE

Wee Willie Winkie
Runs through the town,
Upstairs and downstairs
In his nightgown;
Rapping at the windows,
Shouting through the locks,
"Have the children
Said their prayers?
It's past eight o'clock!"

Except the Lord build the house, they labor in vain that build it: except the Lord keep the city, the watchman waketh but in vain.

—Psalm 127:1

He that dwelleth in the secret place of the most High shall abide in the shadow of the Almighty.

I will say of the Lord, He is my refuge and my fortress: my God; in Him will I trust.

He shall cover thee with His feathers, and under His wings shalt thou trust: His truth shall be thy shield and buckler.

For He shall give His angels charge over thee, to keep thee in all thy ways.

—Psalm 91:1,2,4,11

I will both lay me down in peace, and sleep: for thou, Lord, only makest me dwell in safety.

—Psalm 4:8

## NOW I LAY ME DOWN
## TO SLEEP

Now I lay me down to sleep,
I pray the Lord my soul to keep;
I know He watches over me,
So I can sleep as safe can be!

Thou art worthy, O Lord, to receive glory and honor and power: for thou hast created all things, and for thy pleasure they are and were created.

—Rev. 4:11

Blessing, and honor, and glory, and power, be unto Him that sitteth upon the throne, and unto the Lamb for ever and ever.

—Rev. 5:13

But we see Jesus, crowned with glory and honor.

—Heb. 2:9

On His head were many crowns.

—Rev. 19:12

And I heard as it were the voice of a great multitude, and as the voice of many waters, and as the voice of mighty thunderings, saying, Alleluia: for the Lord God omnipotent reigneth.

—Rev. 19:6

## THE BELLS OF LONDON

Oranges and lemons,
Say the Bells of St. Clements;
God made big red apples,
Say the Bells of Whitechapel;
He made rain and snow
Says the big Bell of Bow;
The world's in His hands
Say the Bells of St. Anne's;
He never will fail me
Say the bells of Old Bailey;
Crown Him with Crowns,
Say the bells over town.

# INDEX

### *Marjorie Ainsborough Decker*

Marjorie Decker is a #1 National Bestseller author who is well-known and loved for her distinct story-telling style.

A native of Liverpool, England, Marjorie now resides in the United States with her husband, Dale. They are parents of four grown sons.

Her Christian Mother Goose® Classics have endeared the trust of parents and the twinkle of children around the world.

Along with authoring ten books in the Christian Mother Goose® Series, Marjorie brings fresh enthusiasm and dynamic teaching to sound, Biblical scholarship. There is a pleasant nostalgia to her children's books with a curious appeal to Bible lovers of all ages . . .

Mrs. Decker is also a conference speaker to adults, a recording artist, and a frequent guest of national network television and radio.